Ellipses

Ellipses

ANDREA MACPHERSON

Clarise Foster, Editor

Signature Editions

Cover design by Doowah Design.
Photo of Andrea MacPherson by John W. MacDonald.

This book was printed on Ancient Forest Friendly paper.
Printed and bound in Canada by Hignell Book Printing Inc.

We acknowledge the support of The Canada Council for the Arts and the Manitoba Arts Council for our publishing program.

Library and Archives Canada Cataloguing in Publication

MacPherson, Andrea, author
Ellipses / Andrea MacPherson.

Poems.
ISBN 978-1-927426-39-5 (pbk.)

I. Title.

PS8575.P465E45 2014 C811'.6 C2014-900947-X

Signature Editions
P.O. Box 206, RPO Corydon, Winnipeg, Manitoba, R3M 3S7
www.signature-editions.com

For our girls
Nora & Taylor
the next generation

And in memory of
May Rowbottom and Gertrude MacPherson

Contents

the other mothers

for May 1926–2005

the genesis of elocution

But I prefer to think of her at seventeen
when words appeared like dreams
to rumble through her mind
and land in her mouth.
Then, she was voracious for the sound of it
the lush jungle of vowels that sank into one another,
the flinty borders of consonants.
These were things she swallowed whole,
savoured like clotted cream on New Year's Day,
to recall as if memory were limitless.

The tip of the tongue, the lips and the teeth.
Walking slowly down Thistle Street
she learned the biology of the mouth:
the tongue, upper jaw, soft palate.
The many, tiny muscles that controlled
each and every word that came from her.
How easily lash could become lathe.
How easily one word could tumble into another.

The seething sea ceaseth, and so the seething sea sufficeth us.
She stepped delicately from one stage to another
collecting with her small medals
(bronze, silver, the flash of plated gold)
that she tucked into boxes,
fleshy velvet sacks,
uneven lengths of jute.
In this way her vocabulary bumped up against industry.
She learned words that her mother had never used,
words that never knew the intimacy of her rolled tongue
and the rumble of voice from somewhere deep in her throat.

In India, individual effort is intensified.

It is impossible to say which of these words
carried her away from the tenement flat.

Perhaps voyage or expedition.
It might have been her caution with the phrases,
the careful movements of her lips as she practiced.
There was always trepidation
fear at the slightest mistake
crumbling the perfection of the words.
As if they were made of nothing more than breath.

Each time she spoke, she travelled to another place:
somewhere across the Atlantic,
into Amazonian jungles, polar ice fields
or someplace more mundane.
A city on another coast,
where the natives carved faces into trees,
knew the names of wind,
the words they whispered.

the gaze

Cobblestones to dirt roads, a wooden walkway if you were lucky; she spent more time looking back, patiently and purposefully grieving the past, while the present slipped away into those dark corners she could never reach. An ocean separated her from her mother's small kitchen table and tarnished kettle, and so she held her hand over the flame of her own stove, the flame leaping. He'd brought her here, where horses were still tethered on the main street and outhouses still stood, crooked and cracking and cruel. She'd stepped backwards instead of forwards and then spent the rest of her life trying to retrace those steps: *How did I get here, how did I get here?*

drifting along the Thompson

The dog with wet snout, fur darker, denser there
and her small body soaked—
white cotton shift made transparent,
pale hair heavy with the river,
and your face at the window when they returned:

Did you search out towels, rush
down the stairs to pull her into your arms?
Or did you pull back
from the window, dip into shadow
leave the dog and the girl to dry in afternoon sun?

Two and a half kilometres to the river,
the path well-worn, well-known—
fishing for rainbow trout with her father,
watching the sun disappear, low on the horizon,
once swimming in even stokes as you watched
from the river's edge, bare legs crossed,
cigarette balanced against ruby lips—
but long, uncertain, now, when she travelled alone.

Later, they would ask you how it happened—
Did you see her go? Did someone else take her?
Do you always allow your two year old to wander alone?
How did the dog pull her out?—
and you remained silent:
still trapped at that window, remembering
her bare feet,
the damp footprints in the grass.

black and white photo, years later

A black party dress, glittering
with sequins at the hem;
a deep neckline and capped sleeves.
1958 and you are radiant.

A Christmas tree still twinkles in the background
suggesting a New Year's Eve party
(bad luck to take the tree down before January 6th,
and you were never one to tempt fate)
some other holiday fete,
compete with coiled hair and red lips.

The red I must imagine for myself,
black and white photos are a trick of memory
a canvas of doubt or possibility.

I imagine you must have danced in the kitchen
nyloned feet gliding across the floor
as your skirt twirled, sparkled, fell into a hush.

Later, it hung in the closet
(still smelling of smoke and perfume,
mixed liquor)
reminding you that—once—
your waist was a whisper of a palm-span,
your shoulders creamy hilltops
that knew the edges of black lace,
the pressure of a man's hand as you danced
hovered, flew.

the other mothers

> You began the women's revolution,
> you were its first martyr.
> I can neither forget you nor tell your story.
> I'll talk instead of myself.
>
> from *September Letters* by Rachel Rose

The other mothers did not understand you,
your brogue too thick, your unhappiness too deep,
your job at the hospital too strange.
And she has a little one at home. Imagine.
Still, you woke early and brushed out your hair
slid your swollen feet into pale, uncomfortable shoes.
The other mothers made beds, scrubbed pots,
while you left the house, stepped into cool halls
not your own for eight long hours.
You began the women's revolution.

They did not know about the days you could not
manage to get out of bed,
the hours you cried for the home you'd left—
your sadness too plain, too predictable,
your husband insisting it would pass.
But it was stubborn, an achey tooth,
inarticulate and misunderstood—nerve damage?
roots?—too painful to bite down on.
Somehow, it stayed with you, refusing to leave:
you were its first martyr.

I did not know you then,
those days when you could not bear
to make your daughter breakfast, hang laundry,
keep her safe in your picketed yard.
I imagine you believed homesickness to be more
than an overused, sentimental expression.
You could not see the life you had—

husband, child, yellow house, motor car—
only the one you had left behind.
I can neither forget you, nor tell your story.

The other mothers did not ask you to tea,
did not whisper about infidelities across phone lines.
They watched you, silent, smoking in the yard
while your daughter turned cartwheels—
Look at me! Look at me!—
and your husband drove taxi, put out fires, hammered nails,
came home with armloads of asparagus as gift.
Before you died, I asked about those years, but received only silence;
now, I see an shadowy affinity between us and so
I'll talk instead of myself.

reading tea leaves

She learned it as a girl in Scotland,
how to turn the cup over
just so
and then three times clockwise
three times opposite.
As simple as the turn of a wrist:
the future spelled out in tea leaves.
(Mine, somehow, always forsees air travel,
a stranger, sad news.
This benign future.)

•

When I am four she reads my tea leaves
in a Chinese restaurant on Kingsway,
as if my entire future rests between her hands.
She turns the porcelaine cup and says, A good one.
Always a good one for me,
not quite so for my mother, who sits quietly with her own cup.
She has stopped finishing her tea at all,
knowing nothing waits for her there.

I never asked who taught her to read leaves,
thought it was more like inheritance—
blue eyes, short legs, round nose—
than anything learned. A strange gift perhaps.

Later, my mother will read leaves at my urging.
She will find a dark man, a surprise, money.
She will turn the cup quickly, leaving behind
a half moon of forgotten tea.
We will not speak her name,
but touch the cooling tea,
leaving our fingertips damp.

solitaire

I lay the cards and think
of you: card table, pot of dark tea,
walls buttered by smoke.

Some days, your nightgown gone stale,
only the sound of cards shuffling.
The slow tick. Something like time slowing.

Easier to lay the cards
than to get up and face the day.
Queen, Jack, ten:
hours pass, cards snapped swiftly back into the deck.
Start again. Start fresh.

Solitaire as lonely as your heart.
You are that last, sad card
unable to find its place.
pushed aside for another deal.
The unending shuffle,
the hope for a new sequence—
a new outcome, future still possible—
the bare sound of card against table.
After all, there is luck in cards.
Shuffle. And shuffle again.

unclaimed

They are unburying the dead at Woodlands.
Make room for condos. Lay new sod.
Plant daffodils and ignore
the upturned dirt in six-foot lengths.
The sight of the river so close,
the iron smell coming up the hill
meeting the dark, deep scent of the earth.

The plaques they'll save.
Move, or auction off.
The unclaimed will simply disappear.

In 1965, you walked the halls of Woodlands,
in a crisp white skirt,
uncomfortable shoes that click-clacked
on the floor.
Passed by closed doors,
wondered at the movement behind them.
Everything just in the periphery,
patients uncertain,
doctors cloaked in silence. Pristine.
One young nurse taken away
after she told them what she'd seen an orderly do—
insane, they whispered, insane.

It was the hissing sound that got you.
Headstones pulled up, reused for walkways and barbeque pits.
Some thrown back in the river,
unwanted fish let go,
sinking quickly, carrying the names with them.

Better, you thought, than Tranquille,
where they'd traded graves for a mass trench.
Better.

In mornings, you made yourself
thick, dark tea,

sat at the small kitchen table
and allowed yourself those moments:
sun barely cresting the horizon,
hot tea steaming,
still in only your slip.
You waited for the last moment
to dress, button your pressed skirt,
push your feet into sensible white shoes—
to let the day become inevitable.

The hospital set on the hill,
once the lunatic asylum,
now simply a place for those unwanted.
Unwanted, finally, seemingly a kind word.
Retarded, not right, moron;
all these names slipped out too easily; daily.

Later, you said you liked the way
they wanted to hold your hand,
how they were happy to follow you
down the halls; simple, you said,
there's nothing strange, just simple.

You've been gone too long now,
for me to ask if you knew those children
whose headstones have long sunk
to the river's bed,
whose names are committed to no paper,
who are still unwanted,
unclaimed.

Or, if they would remember
your tidy white skirt,
your heavy brogue
your hands, fingers splayed,
leading them forward.

a day in February with my grandmother

Today, we listen as the blue jay cries:
a sound too loud, too hard for this clear day;
instead there should be the gentle rustling of a more quiet bird
a bird less constrained by needs
the possibility of scavenging
blue feathers.

We will step away from this small white house,
trees filled with blue jays and wind chimes,
and into a clinic; into a place where
the word white takes on a new meaning.
There is no talk of the new lumps
appearing on my grandmother's body;
hair is brushed over the largest crest
until it might only be a curl of grey.

When she moves, it is slowly,
methodically
as she grasps my arm. She speaks to me about nothing, everything:
about absence and the fluidity of the long, blue sky
about her new, voracious desire for sleep and, sometimes, pastry.
I imagine the flakes on her fingertips,
the memory of sugar and thick, warm custard on her lips.

Later, she will put her head on the kitchen table and sleep;
she will let herself breathe and dream,
the warmth of the room around her
like an old, patched shawl.

3 am March 2, 2005

And what was I doing in that moment?
Sleeping (the first time in weeks)
in a soft bed, the scent of wilted lilies in the room
my husband's arm heavy against my hip;
normalcy redefined, flattened out and breathless.

Eleven days before
you saw your mother and called out
to her
though she had been gone almost sixty years—
her lungs as well,
pink to black and back, recomposing—
and what did I think in that moment?
Release. The quick snap of relief
of familiar faces and voices,
her brogue there with you in the hospital room.
That the light must be white-hot,
that you must think her beautiful.

When the phone rang—
fumble, quickening of heart
(is it possible for that to be hereditary too?
Weak heart, heartless, faltering)
the words caught.
And in that moment
I remembered everything about you:
cobbled streets and high black heels,
your face upturned to Polynesian sun
(large, movie-star glasses and pixie cut)
smoke
songs I did not recognize in the kitchen
(sunlight—the back southern window)
a tiny glass of Tia Maria, the smudge of your lips
and your voice, your voice
your voice
speaking to your mother again.

rose: thirty-odd years later

The full explosion of yellow to orange
back again
climbing up the back wall—
once drifting to cover the back porch
curling over the railing:
small hands, spike of them
bright drop of blood
(reminding me, now, of Bluebeard).

It came from Germany,
a small stalk
only the promise of its scent
lacy edges of bloom
from the faded society newspaper,
the spots where the words had been rubbed off:
her hands holding the edge
face pressed close,
pleasure plain to see.

Now, the tree climbs past window line
angling for roof and beyond:
he pulls the branches low
cuts as many as he can,
will later set the blooms on a table,
let the scent fill the room,
remember her face as it had been then.

the rocking chair

There had been a complicity once,
a certain comfort and absolution to days marked by routine,
the sound of the TV turned up loud,
perhaps a cough, a sigh when rising.
That will be what he misses most:
the possibility of an exhalation
just there
the creak from her chair when it rocked.
The chair is threadbare,
showing years of material
flowers, plaid, an unrecognizable beige
detailing fifty-nine years by pattern
and years of a slow, steady rock
the memory of a body made lighter, still.

moving day, forty years later

Then, there had been tidy cardboard boxes
a truck piled high
and the coil of cigarette smoke in the air
marking it: mine. Home.

Now, take the lead-glass window
(dining room, east wall)
that once held the reflection of ice cubes in tumbler
her hand strumming the edge
the party going on around her—
your sister, already drunk,
telling stories of a mother you never knew
slurring, grasping the table for balance
before the inevitable crash
crystal slipping from table lip.

Remove the glass doorknobs
and slip them into your pocket:
keep safe
the memory of opening and closing
quiet in the morning while she slept,
louder—later—after a quarrel,
after a hole has been burned in the carpet
or you've forgotten to cut down fresh lilacs
the cut-glass vase waiting. Empty.

Pull up the cement steps
painted pale grey now,
but, then, a startling red
under the hem of your daughter's wedding gown,
her slow wave from the top,
just before the descent.

Pack carefully—
tissue, towels, wool blankets—

tuck it all away
until there are only bare plaster walls,
the memory of hooks and handprints,
the smudge of her uncertain hands
down the stairwell.
Take those as well.

sixteen months

I dream of you.
Or, rather, of guilt and grief
the messy entanglements there,
conjoined twins: sharing bone and flesh.

I dream of burning cigarettes
emeralds cased in gold
dark, plain shoes
and the days before the funeral
when I thought, *I knew.*

I knew it like the ache in a muscle rarely used:
nameless, shifting,
but present.
Since you said you knew it would come to this;
you had always known.

I do not dream of those eleven days
when I held your hand,
slept curled like a snail,
listened for breath.
Instead of white corridors
you asked for hemlock—
your own bed—
and we could not even give you that.

routine

for Gertrude 1914—2009

Quill Lake in spring

The night your father died,
you dreamed you would never see him again.

You had been in the sanatorium for two years then,
sleeping on an open porch when warm,
a lump of wax lodged in your lung to try to expel the tuberculosis.
From the porch you could see a lake,
frozen and silver in winter, tepid in spring
and perhaps this is why you dreamed of him at his home on Quill Lake.
The proximity of water turning you clairvoyant.

•

Your mother died at your birth, leaving your father
with three small blonde children.
There is a photo of her pregnant
with you,
your father tall and moustached behind her:
your brother and sister in starched shirts on her knee,
and you, hidden beneath linen skirts, present nonetheless.

After her death, you lived on a farm with a kind man and his wife.
Your father visited, and you remember him bringing you sweets,
the stains they left on his hands.
Once you visited your father at Quill Lake with his segmented family:
his second wife and their twenty-one children.
You walked with him along the periphery of the lake,
your feet almost touching the blue.

harvest, 1945

Metallic scent high in her nose when she bends to till,
no need to check gusset—
she knows there will be heavy, dark blood that seems to cry,
No baby no baby no baby!
Already thirty, too old to be childless
her body unwelcoming
(she does not yet know there will be the three boys
in quick succession, wearing her thin
wearing her out in ways she could not imagine).
Now, only, that she'll wring her underpants in the sink while her husband sleeps,
ashamed of the sight of her blood.
From the open window, though,
the beginnings of spring in the trees,
those fallow fields beyond
forever stretching,
harvest yet to come.

farmhouse: Winnipeg

Her hand over the stove burner
still warm—memory of gas, flame—
the light of the afternoon coming
through the back window
ladders of light on the pine floor,
the knots eyeholes
to the cellar below.

There, neat rows of canned fruit—
peach, blueberry, raspberry, saskatoons—
glowing despite the damp and dark.
Her hands learned the shelves—
could navigate them in the deepest dark—
finding slim slivers in fingerpads
later to be abandoned on flat surfaces
butcher block, end table, radio.
The house cluttered with them
small haystacks
echoing the landscape outside

flat prairie fields
long fencelines

further—barn

paint peeling
crumbling in her hands.
Endless.

Her world this tight:
wheat to the left
lazy cattle to the right
and her palms pressed to wooden shelves
just for the pinch of sliver.

Saskatoon Sanatorium, 1940

Sight of the lake from the window, cots on the open-air porch, starched bed linens crisp against palms. Other girls her age dancing to "A Nightingale Sang in Berkeley Square" and she is having wax lodged in her lung—scars like pale, flattened earthworms—and listening to the girl next to her talking about a fiancé, babies, the future. All she can see is the ebb of the lake, the way the lights turn on in houses, across the bay. The familiarity of a home, the word so thick. The san, the san, the san. She knows the girl will not make it, knows many of them will never leave the sanatorium. This lake view will be the end. This blue, this blue.

vows, 1946

Slate blue dress, red flowers at her breast. The word husband chalky in her mouth. He'll wear his uniform of course; they will smile, only glance at one another from the corners of their eyes. Later, she'll take off a heel, hold it in her hand as he folds his pants, turns his back to her as he undresses. Between them, the reminder that she was not the first; she was lucky to live, to grieve, to console. Lucky to pin the red rose at her chest, to wear his ring.

(In summers, they visit the girl's grave. She brings flowers, though she no longer remembers the girl's voice on the porch of the san. But he wilts, he cries. And she stands tall.)

routine, 1951

Heft, pull, pin, pin. Sheets on the line. Underpants. Sleepers. Cotton shift. Slip. Baskets overflow, white in the dazzling sun—baskets never empty, the bottom only a future possibility. Four boys and her, all tiny pants and smaller socks, toes in need of darning. Heft, pull, pin, pin. Bottles to wash, pots to scrub, dinners to make, hurts to soothe: the boys too close in age, her husband too aware of failures, her own resolve weakening, faltering. These moments, pinning the laundry to the line with the hypnotic motion of wrists and arms, are hers alone; so little, now, so much less than she'd hoped for. A view of the flat fields beyond, the pale yellow house, her own hands strong and knotted and chapped. But the boys, those three small boys in short pants and trim haircuts; the boys. Heft, pull, pin, pin.

empty, 1977

Shadows and smudges on bedroom walls where once there were denim trousers, balled socks, stacks of schoolbooks, a ball. A bat. The boys now sleeping next to young wives in bungalows and apartments filled with baby blankets. Knit bonnets, ribbons she'd sewn on. Keeping hands busy. They visit, place fair babies on her lap. She touches their temples, remembers. But mostly, there is the deep quiet of the house—the jangle of his teacup on saucer, her hands in soapy water, washing two plates, two cups, two spoons. In the garden, she plants snapdragons against the carport, saddened by the way they double, twine.

descent, 1983

When they take his toes, she knows it will never be the same. Now: canes, walkers, hand rails, the whirr of a bed that lifts. Separate rooms. Tea at opposite ends of the table. Slow shuffle, loss of words, days filled with silence. The shape of days changes. She bakes pies that remain untouched. Looks out windows that remain closed. Things crumble. She remains.

Gertrude at ninety–one

Suddenly aged:
fear perhaps
(inability to catch her breath
vertigo, the suggestion of something cardiac)
or all those years catching up

a sanatorium; a farm; a city;
two fingers of rye (no, three);
a long, slow death;
the air on her face in the early afternoon.

Now, white hair appears
and hands grasp at walls to steady:
push back, push away what's to come.
There is still the cry of a sparrow in morning
still the view of water from your window.

ninety-four

September 1914

How quickly we forget the fickle nature
of blood: pumping, coursing
just as quickly turning to still pools,
a thick skin on top, heavy cream in a jar.

Nothing gentle about the morning—
coming faster, stronger—
the long afternoon—*push, push*
can't stop the bleeding—
or the evening. Endless. Still. Silent.

No one notices you in the bassinette
tiny, dark haired, docile;
they are too busy with the intricacies of mourning,
with heavy cotton sheets,
closing her eyes.

February 2009

Between Nicola Valley and Peachland,
snow: icing sugar on hemlock, fir
and a thick swath of red, cut
up the ridge, strict line at the edge of road.
Soon, bare pine branches, trunks silvered
when they cut the trees open,
delicate lacing, bands of shivering blue.
They'll call it beautiful,
awed by the ability to insidiously creep
a slow murmuring of end.

shadowlands

for the others

Ophelia swims the river

What if, instead, you swam;
pulled cupped river water
downstream
felt the tug of current;
pushed
white gown billowing
grazing gills and algaed rock
bloated with liquid memory,
drowned song in bleached linens
until you reached the Port of Elisnore;
the small harbour, the pier
masts billowing, wood creaking—
groaning, alive.

And there you would dry yourself off—
hope for sunshine , but settle
for anything; too long submerged.
Look across the sound,
imagine a different sort of life.

Change your name.
Cut your hair.
Take to singing in the choir.

Do not look back.

bathing

on the drawing Children's Bath in the Garden by Suzanne Valadon, 1910, crayon & pencil on paper

If you imagine the tree swaying,
you might hear the wind:
see how the leaves shiver,
lean low and consider.

Perhaps the woman bent over the tub—
steel, certainly, the scrub of it
in the wild grass—
reminds you of your mother:
she, too, knew the intimacy of bathing,
of someone else's pale shirts and underpinnings,
washed and scrubbed them
until her hands were red and raw.

She has positioned the tub
away from prying eyes,
under this tree in the grove;
she does not look up, does not remind
that her hands once bathed
your small shoulders,
that spot in the small of your back
you could never reach
once scooped errant leaves
from your bathwater:
held everything clear.

The Blue Room

Suzanne Valadon's oil on canvas, 1923

reclining, only
not plaiting her hair
pulling up stockings or staring
in a mirror
blue flowers the only witness

a stack of books
a lit cigarette
Sunday afternoon
with the washing done
the apartment quiet

listening only to the petals folding
unfurling
crushed beneath her elbow

La Toilette

taken from Henri de Toulouse-Lautrec's oil on canvas, 1889

My knees are what ache
cartilage and bone
unrepentant bitter lovers.

Even now, I cannot straighten them;
the black stockings will stay.
Two chairs, unmade bed
one copper bathtub: all I have.

The white petticoats don't count
(they are for them—
tall hats, slim moustaches,
walking sticks, folded francs)
nor the black stockings;
only the coil of hair at my nape,
the way I twist my wrist to tuck it away
leaving a clear view:
their faces, the curl of lip
anonymity momentarily broken
by my gaze.

Medical Inspection (Rue des Moulins)

taken from Henri de Toulouse-Lautrec's oil on cardboard, 1894

It's the thighs that make them vulnerable.

Skirts hitched to waist,
black stockings keeping kneecaps modest,
and the creamy back of thigh,
unfamiliar with sunlight or rainstorms
now revealed:
each crease, freckle or flaw—
red path of wild cat's scratch,
raw, round marker of burning tip
of cigarette—
doubled in the light.

This is why they only look forward,
the past an open palm,
an elderly nurse's dirty fingernails,
an unknown man's breath.

(Instead the innocence
of the spine—look where it meets collar
where it still hides.)

Equestrienne (at the Circus Fernando)

from Toulouse-Lautrec's 1888-1889 oil on canvas

If not for the fall
she would be perched there still:
sidesaddle, delicate bones
of ankles crossed
creating that X
marker for sightline, pain.
A break—shatter—
crushed bones beneath
paneled tent: red, yellow, red
blood on earthen floor darkening beneath her.
Her palms—fingers splayed—
a reminder of momentum,
the sheer brilliance of gravity.

(Later—another tent,
another flash of ankle,
but not hers: pale,
unfractured.)

Horsehair: mane, bristles,
how a brush can speak,
hold the past in each stroke.

how we define voluntary

on Camille Claudel and Montdevergues Asylum

Marble or bronze:
always the sway of back,
as if the spine came unhinged
instead curled like a snail—
something that moves slowly,
languid
leaving a shimmering trail in its wake
dancers' bodies, surely
the song just there behind them.

Those years buzzing,
brimming with the sound of bees
swarming: beating wings,
so like a heartbeat.
Vertumnus and Pomona
Sakuntala, The Waltz.
Hands busy.

Each sculpture with reaching arms,
as you must have reached,
the white lace at your shoulder twisted,
dark hair coming free from clasp;
you push it away,
your hands sore, red.

And after
what did your hands look like?
Soft, milky, unused
plucking at the petals of a wildflower
(found in the hospital garden
pale white against all the green,
your sight not changed, your eye as keen)
while your brother sat across from you
referred to you in the past tense:
        She was. You were.

in Bluebeard's basement

And what if, instead,
you found a gallon of bleach in the basement—
perched on laundry tub,
abandoned with his white shirts
in a bunch—
and scrubbed the key until your fingers
were raw:
the scalded red of them startling
but domestic enough;
his white shirts in the laundry tub still.

You would come to hate the scent of bleach—
medicinal, chemical,
reminiscent of your eighth grade class
when they made you pin a frog
to dissection board,
forced you to lift scalpel,
cut through grainy skin—
and you would resist the urge
to try the doorknob again
curiosity deadened, now,
pushed aside like a rotting apple,
forgotten like breadcrumbs or an early morning dream
when you passed it in the hallway
your arms full of undershirts,
trousers, pajamas,
white collared shirts, the cuff stained with blood.

without windows

for Barbara Newhall Follett

Dear Barbara,

Where did you go with those thirty dollars? Out into a cold night, your shoes too thin, a purple scarf wrapped loosely around your neck. Only your notebook in your pocket, words inked in, scratched out. Not prepared for what came next. Never prepared for what had come before. Did he stand by the window and watch you go? Worse, perhaps.

Your silence after the answer.

The break might have happened years before, after your father left, your words run dry. Child prodigy: a taunt. Your life turned loose, eleven years lonely for him, language lost. Did you save those thirty dollars, pin them into a soft, old bra, and wait? A night promising snow, tracks impossible.

absent in the spring
for Agatha Christie

Those eleven days are yours.
The days you didn't acknowledge, didn't speak of
didn't write about.
They are yours alone.
I don't wonder why you used her name,
if you carefully mimicked her script,
touched your necklace as she would have.
Her gestures were already committed to your memory.

I don't wonder what you meant.

But there was Rosalind, too small
too small to know infidelity,
to understand what leaving meant;
too small to understand fame.
Maybe you apologized, held her tight in your arms,
told her you'd missed her,
would never leave her,
thought only of her while you were gone.
Wrote a story for her;
just for her.
Or perhaps you only bought her taffy,
a creamy shell
a jar full of sand.

how would you know it was love?

for Sylvia, February 11, 1963

Because she left them pitchers of milk
and soft, white bread
must have bent to kiss their sweaty, sleep-creased foreheads
straightened a blanket, and stayed
a moment longer than she had intended,
would have known they'd wake hungry
and without her.

Because there was a taped door,
an open window despite February's chill,
and her knees would have been cold on the kitchen floor,
quickly turning an angry red.

Because the baby nurse and the carpenter were dependable sorts,
scheduled to arrive early—
before the children woke,
while the sky was still grey and cold and cruel,
waiting impossibly for the light.

dreamless

for Shura Hughes, March 29, 1969

Because Assia taped the doors, too
turned on the gas as well,

but pulled Shura close, pretended
it would be as simple as sleep.

Storyville, 1912

taken from an untitled photo by EJ Bellocq

What is left, then?
Only breast, slope of stomach
the dark triangle
between her legs—
behind,
the fireplace unlit
and the door barred
with dresser, locks, wire—
nothing but dark
gaping hole of mouth in song.

(Not Ave Maria
no hymns or hums
that speak to cathedrals,
to that slim line:
Virgin or whore.)

Her face now only a black slash—
regret, a wish for anonymity or something else:
the indecency of the female body,
the shame of these photos,
of his art—their bodies so plainly sinful.
A Jesuit priest's sensibilities
in the way she is blinded,
beheaded
rage there in the depth
of the groove.

posing for Bellocq

His mind is a flurry—*take off the stockings, lock the door, help me push the dresser over, we'll block the door*—and he'll tie wire to the handle, pull tight, forget me for a moment—*here, Bellocq, I'm standing by the dresser, in front of all those queer collages*—and now what? *Turn left, a bit more, angle your head away, I want to see the locket*—if I turn this far, there's the crick in my neck, my shoulders hurt, the room's too cold (does he ever light the fire?) Flash of the bulb—*I wasn't ready*—a second. *Put your arm on the mantle, bend it, I want to see the point of your elbow.* There's rain outside, I can hear it against the glass. Another flash. Another. Turn my torso. Put my hand behind my back. The locket feels heavy, warm now against my chest. Are we finished yet? *A few more, then a glass. I promise.*

photo: mother and child

Could it be the scarf
at your throat? The polka-dot pattern
somehow offensive—
too whimsical, too obvious,
too feminine?
Or the smooth sheen
of your light hair, parted
low on the side?

Her eyes are hard—sidelong—
watching you
when she should be smiling,
her gaze directed at the photographer.
Instead: furrowed brow
side profile, lips tight—
pursed, unhappy, controlled.
Not the gaze of a mother,
yet the gaze of your mother.

You hold the smallest child's hand
your pinkie lost
in the small fist
and perhaps this is why—
you hold close the things she has lost.

motherhood: another sort

A child in the garden—
sunlight, certainly,
a border of begonias
(or snapdragons, it does not matter)
a blue tricycle on its side—
and a mother in the upstairs bedroom,
the curtains drawn,
damp cloth across her forehead
an empty glass—
remnants of gin, sharp scent
of pine
filling the room.

Migraines, melancholy, malaise;
all the words taste foreign
something bitter at the back of the throat.
It is simpler to see:
bed sheets rumpled, in need
of airing
cigarette stubbed out, left
on bedside table where it once burned
her body curled, bent
into itself, around nothing—
only the blessed empty landscape
of the bed, the darkness,
the quiet.

While outside—
a small arch, lifted
running,
the sun hard on the eyes,
loud on the grass.

the things we buried

I

The shining jewel button
from my grandmother's sweater;
small, quick hands
thread unraveled and then tucked away—
the shimmer kept safe (momentarily)
in my pocket. Feel the rub
of it against my palm all day.
Imagine its secret sparkle.

Wordless when she asks me
to search for the missing button.
It's always something, she says,
and I understand this means more than I realize.
Stare, instead, at the bare expanse of wool
thread dangling, button missing,
hands worrying.

II

You buried the poodle in the backyard,
under the apple tree, you said,
but everyone concerned about the fruit,
proximity to death.
Would the apples be mealy,
browned, rotten right through?
So, instead you found a quiet corner
and buried him late at night,
alone.
They slept and you dug,
foregoing shovel for bare hands
wanting the feel of the earth to be your last
memory of him.

III

A baby.
Tiny coffin, plain wood.
All the memories: the booties,
the pale bonnet, the soft, worn blanket.
What would they have said,
watching the earth swallow the pine box?
There would be no marker,
no long, tearful elegy,
soon, no one left to remember,
only the mound of dirt,
greedy.

Oregon, 1953

Less than three months,
they drive down the coast:
her hand is tight and stiff on the armrest
her eyes straight ahead and dull blue.

    She might be dreaming about the sandbars there
    or the tall redwoods huddled together like shy schoolchildren.
    She might be reconsidering, after all.

He drives, the road smooth and seamless
beneath the hum of the tires. He is only thinking
of the next rest stop; the sandwiches and lemonade
she has packed in the back seat. As if it were a holiday.

Oregon is colder than she imagined:
the tight steel blue of the sky reminiscent of grief.
She had expected something else,
some other memory to carry home with her.
    Not this hollowness.

When they talk about it, they call it *the procedure*,
careful to dance around the technical names.
This way, it is easier to forget about the metal probing between her legs
and his stony face in the waiting room.

•

She wants to drive on the way back,
hungry for something beneath her fingertips,
the swift, certain roll of the road under the tires.
She drives until her eyes become blurred
and trees begin to resemble swaying limbs.
Their lips are sealed
tight like new jars of summer jam.

At a rest stop she calls her son;
his voice is thin over the line, impatient to play outside,
uncertain of why his mother suddenly cries
her voice echoing in the metal phone booth.

shadowlands

for J

I

He kicked his legs in the bath only hours before—
delight! delight!—
and so this can not be what you've come to.

Cold hospital corridors,
closed doors, antiseptic rooms
where they tell you to wait, to weep
to wail.

No one acknowledges the fury,
how your hands won't be still, but fret
finding nothing, now,
to keep them busy.
Fury comes fast and hard,
a bottomless well.

The bath still warm,
perhaps edging towards cooling.
They say you can drown in an inch of water.
You know it's much less than this.

II

Loss is all sharp angles, surprising corners
edges that bite the tender places.
And so there are no words of comfort,
only your sharp shoulder bones against the black silk of your dress
offering no hiding places,
no shadowlands, no refuge.

The service whispers and howls and keens
while you keep your body still, head bent low,
your want for composure, the necessity of folded hands
knuckles turning white, strained.

God called him home.
    Hollow words.
    Hymns are flat.
    Language lost.
    You have questions for God.

This loss all encompassing,
the deepest, darkest ocean of grief:
the bottom unseen,
and I am left with the guilt of those spared,
my child safely at home,
tucked in, tucked away.

•

I cannot write about your grief;
words demand more than I can give.
I can't imagine your sorrow
the depth and breadth of it
Your sorrow must seem easier to give in,
wade further and further away from the self you once knew,
from the shape you imagined your life would be.
Now, drowned. Still drowning.
The same sinking I felt when I touched your hand,
understood why you needed to hold yourself still and straight,
pulling against the awful undertow.

III

This pond is too deep
too vast—
you push against the muddy waters,
feels its algaed threads against your hands
and only tread, tread
until your legs burn and your heart
considers shattering.
Or, shatters again.

You know you will sink. This slick bottom
the last home you know.
This is inevitable, from this there is no recovery.

You've heard of the dredgers
men who slip in slick and black,
find what has long ago been lost.
You wonder what they would find here,
if they would claim your body as evidence
or a casualty;
either way, you would be lifted,
body bloated by sorrow,
pulled free of this water, this endless depth,
and reach the thin, fresh air once again.

directions for sleep

for mine

version two

My mother and I argue over baked goods.
She insists she baked when I was young—
cookies, tarts, pies, shortbread, cakes—
but I have no memory
of measuring sugar,
watching chocolate melt in silver pans,
rolling out a pie crust slowly.
No memory of honey and raisins warming,
the scent of apple filling the house.
Nor sticky fingers (after)
crumbs to collect on the butcher block.

But I did, she says. There was.

I remember long expanses of blue water,
stepping carefully over linoleum seams,
collecting acorns in an orange bucket.
Once, her pressing money into the hands
of a neighbour: *Go, take you and the kids away. Back to Ireland.*
Only their absence, later, on the playground.

One version full of sweetness,
the nostalgic ingredients for butter tarts
or angel food cake,
surely the things a small child catalogues,
draws upon years later when considering
words like wool, puzzle or dawn.

Yet the other version mine alone—
the sharp smell of metal on palms
after holding the swing's chain too tightly,
the girl taken and returned damaged, changed,
my belief that stepping on a crack
would do irreparable harm.
No shortbread or oatmeal cookies in those versions—
no sweetness left behind.

summer of 1983

From the right lane, from nowhere,
a black van
all bright lights, tires crunching on ice,
and the momentary panic too well known:
black panel van,
omen, harbinger of all those evil deeds
of childhood.

Black panel vans—
parks, schoolyards, swimming pools.
A lost puppy, a broken leg,
your mother sent me.
Black panel vans—
scavengers. Touching down only
where small girls might be,
all pigtails and coloured ribbons,
freshly scrubbed faces, gleaming.

Before the sightings of black panel vans,
middle aged men with dark eyes,
reports of girls lured, girls lost—
paper bags, once simply for ham sandwiches,
sectioned pieces of ripe mandarin oranges,
now something sinister, complicated—
our childhoods were simple,
benign stretches of kick the can,
plastic dolls and vibrant front lawns,
skipping ropes on hot asphalt driveways.
A complacency to our innocence;
everything shrouded in that golden glow.

The after:
after the girl was taken to the abandoned field,
after our mothers realized they knew her—
Girl Guide meetings, bake sales, *oh god, her mother—*

after doors were abruptly locked,
conversations whispered,
block parent stickers appeared in windows.
The yellow and red of it a reminder:
a declaration of protest.

Black panel vans. Phone calls
to police stations at every sighting.
Black panel vans everything evil.

And now, the van passes me on the right,
moves as slick and calm as an eel in night water,
leaving behind no trace,
only the reminder of what once was,
and what was lost.

eight

Fifty-six days and still you are an abstract:
algebra, pi, gravity—
nothing certain
not bread rising in a hot oven,
not the groove of pen to paper,
not even the angle of my elbow in sleep.

I imagine this is something else inherited—
an inability to believe
in the want of the body.
Reproduce, reproduce—
the concept turned didactic,
foreign.
And so I think of the women before me,
their own cloudy disbelief
(too young, too old, not ready)
so like mine,
yet separate in want:

The twenty-year-old with a tiny infant slipping
from her unconscious form;
the thirty-year-old bending low,
holding the bulk of her stomach while grasping
hay, wheat, small boys in dust.

Or the others who held fast to denial
forgot names, dates,
pretended that the pure white gusset
of underpants was hopeful.
Named their children,
gave them fathers, stepped away.

Waded in the abstract,
swallowed it like early morning gin.

three

Your birth:
silence.

Those moments too long,
the echoing emptiness of the doctors' quiet
your voice not yet learned.

Three times, the cord
around your neck—
a trinity of ropey tightness,
the impossibility of breath
had it been any other way.

The doctor says, Someone is looking out for you,
and I immediately know:
two grandmothers (veterans of childbirth,
one mercifully knocked out, the other excruciatingly
awake, aware of each child leaving her body)
looking down on the operating room,
watching the incision across hipline,
your tiny face suddenly appearing.

Then, your cry:
the most pure, dazzling sound I have ever heard.
A girl, a girl,
even though everyone was certain you would be a boy,
a girl lifted and placed on my chest.
A girl I'd spoken to over those long months,
my girl, as certain and perfect as the day's sun,
as the women looking down on you.

maps

After you were born,
my back held a map
all purple ink borders
that breadcrumb trail from childhood stories:
here, my spine. Here, the space in between where they put the needle.
I didn't expect this strange chart,
was caught by its presence when I slowly undressed
to step into the shower,
cautious already of the heat on tender skin,
afraid to look at the bandaged scar low across my stomach.
There, in strange purple shorthand down my spine,
a whole world—
the place that had been just me before
and became us after.

ode: infant

It snowed while we slept,
you and I,
and I held you at the window to look—
the back lane a stretch of white,
the rooftops capped with icing,
the chill of the afternoon coming through the glass.
You stared, all that white new to you,
another unknown.

Only two-and-a-half months ago there was sun
a bright, late summer's day when you were born
and freshly cut roses lining the window sill.

It seemed time moved more quickly now
the months tumbling into one another,
marked only by hours of sleep,
the reach of your arms.
Roses to snow to roses again.

But for now, your eyes wide,
cheek pressed against mine,
winter pulled taut between us,
a reminder of long seasons still to come.

hair elegy

Air insistent at the nape of my neck
before now unknown:
for thirty-three years,
hair worn long
(covering breasts, at least—
once, touching curve of waist)
and now this sudden, strange sensation:
shorn.

Now, hair disappeared
migrated, protested
after your birth—
the newness of your tiny body
something to rail against,
the body turning against itself.
Mornings, I woke
to hair covering the pillow,
pulled strands from the drain,
found my hands full.
Lamenting.
Keening at the loss.
Once, perhaps, it could have been
a hair shirt,
could have foretold pain and betrayal.

Now, only the sharpness of separation—
your body from mine,
hair from scalp—
of all the things that cannot be resumed,
cannot be stitched whole.

incision, incisive

They cut me hip to hip
and now, thirty months later,
I still feel it: raised scar,
the place where life began.
Earthworms. Silken ribs. That perfect scar.
I do not want it to fade:
my last visceral memory of you
before we were separated—
when you were still a part of me.
An extension, or more.

Others say that this scar makes me a failure
that—somehow—your birth
and my motherhood are diminished.
They cluck their tongues,
disapprove:
Well, you didn't really. You haven't, really.
Birth is one-dimensional.

As if splitting is the barometer for love
or dedication.
The needle in my spine,
the layers of muscle bisected
do not count:
there was no pushing,
no tearing, no spidery stitches.
They want me to feel only shame.

Instead, pride pulses at this choice:
the knowledge that this was my first act
of protection.
That I instinctively knew the way it should be.
    And that I saved you—

three times around her neck,
so tight, had it been
any other way—
and that their judgment is tinny and cold,
full of only angry fear,
smoldering.

writing lessons

I want to write you poems
but it seems all I see is the sweetness
the goodness
and these things, they say, are not interesting
much like laundry or clear skies.
The domestic still held separate,
only ever at the periphery: soft focus.
Romanticized.

I could write about the feel of baby bottles
in soapy water,
the new, clean fear for my daughter
in even the mildest situations;
the sleep that does not come,
the love that burrows and burrows
until it is at the exact core.

The edge of sorrow has rubbed off,
leaving pages bare
the domestic—motherhood and all its messes—
is not the stuff of poetry.

turning the clocks ahead

When the clocks broke ahead—
pushing past, into the future
and what was still to be—
the morning unfolded slowly,
skies full of dim light
the dark remaining a moment too long.

The baby slept.
And I thought about books
I would never write—
words I would never string together
in that half-magical way—
books that would remain only in my periphery
never truly appearing.

Once, I wrote a list
of books I was planning to write,
a list of books to complete by age thirty.
Greying ink now, the page turned soft,
the list incomplete.

Those unfinished, unwritten books
I will not write.
Words have been taken,
all used up by daily utterances:
Mama, book, sock, Dada.
The words had come.
Yes, I thought them,
spoke them even,
but I did not write them down.

The baby sighs, moans softly,
and I'm aware that the day will be spent
wading in words—
lately, school, and button—
but that my page will remain blank.

I will give her all these words happily,
with great, greedy pleasure,
but still wonder where my own words have gone.
If the clocks had shifted again,
and stolen them quickly away into the future.

The day will resume.
We'll get up, go about our routine—
slicing bananas, reading *Curious George*,
napping on puffed white pillows—
all the predictable, perfect moments of the day,
and another hour will slide ahead,
move forward,
pushing towards morning.
I'll wonder when the words will come,
when they might settle stubbornly upon the page,
not yet able to acknowledge the words I've spoken,
the words I've given her, have been the right ones.

search party

A pocket full of notes—
lines of poems,
descriptions of characters' fingers,
brief sketches of dialogue.
This is what you would find in my winter
coat, folded pages tumbling
out like new autumn leaves
the sound of them—
balled up, shoved in pocket,
put away—
so like those same leaves
beneath our feet.

All those moments caught by pen
hastily scrawled and then tucked away.
Nothing perfect. Nothing perfect enough.
Later, they could be pasted together
made into some strange collage
of my thoughts:
blue, ocean, peony
dark, almost, sigh.

What would you believe of me then?
A poet of sorrows,
a pen made only for thieved stories
long-forgotten whispers in dim rooms.
Would you search out those words
the indentations of my pen
below your fingertips?
Find my voice in those words,
solace in the sound
of pages flattened out again.

bed landscape

The bed has turned into a playground
for the baby's dolls and stuffed animals

lost pacifiers, tangled blankets,
abandoned socks, pajamas pulled off in the night.

Once, we slept.
Once, we lay here together

skin moist, breathless
after we'd made love.

Once, I'd wake alone
to grey skies and listen for rain,

the sound of it clear
in the quiet of the house.

When was that?

All those months so distant,
unfamiliar in a bracing way.

Now, damp sheets are pulled off,
laundered clean again.

directions for sleep

(variations from an insomniac)

I

Lie completely still, on your side
or on your back. Never on your stomach;
you might breathe in another's dreams.

II

Leave a notepad beside your bed
perhaps a quill-tipped pen.

Ignore words like bluebells, marina, sorrow;
they have no place here.

III

Imagine yourself on a deserted beach.
long lines of blue sea uninterrupted,
the wind coming from the west.

Do not think of sharks, your childhood
fear of seaweed tangling
or the time you were six and stung
by a jellyfish, its transparency unfair.

IV

Think of the yard on 54th Street,
when you lay on the grass
sunwarmed, patchworked by leaves from the acorn tree.
Do not remember when the neighbour girl
cut her palm so deep you understood
why crimson was not red—
the time the boy next door hit you
so hard you did not cry,
taught you something
about the cruelty of men—
or how the Irish woman down the road
packed up her children and her suitcase,
used money from your mother
Take it, take it and go
for an early morning flight back
while her husband rubbed sleepy, hard eyes.

V

Do not wonder why you have never
purchased a thesaurus,
learning the difference between eminent and immanent
(because it will not matter)
pressing your face into the scent of ink and word
as you have done since you were a small child.

VI

Place the back of your hand over your eyes,
hoping to seal in darkness and force sleep to come.

You should not remember the small room
in your grandmother's basement ,
dark and lined with preserves—

blueberry, strawberry, apricot—
or the way another basement across the city
came out into sunlight
into a garden tumbling away with itself,
a garden from a children's tale
choking with lilac and roses and apple trees,
their branches gnarled and entwined.

VII

Consider how your leg might twitch,
anxious, too, for sleep:
a comfort in the night, not quite a stranger.

VIII

Develop a nightly ritual:
meditate, spray your pillow with lavender, read a book.
Forget about the words, though,
the way they move—muscular—across the page;
do not let your mind wander to your own incomplete
poems, the one about silver birches
the way your hand curls around a pen,
the moment when the line is complete, and the perfection
of the comma.

IX

Concentrate on your breathing,
deeply in, slowly out. Be aware of the rise and fall.

This is not the time to think about salt water,
holding your breath until you were sure
your tender pink lungs would implode,
opening your eyes in the grainy blue

to see a dead fish below you—
red and yellow, too calm, too still—
when you had been hoping for rough coral,
perhaps a lost bracelet winking in the sand.

X

Place a glass of water on your nightstand:
room temperature, tepid.
Close off the way the water was flat and stretched
out to the lip of the cliff in St. Andrews,
the reflection there of the boy who jumped
from the bell tower,
the way the sand sucked at your hand
when you pushed it down—
surprised by the split of cold.

XI

Repeat a mantra if you must:
reassure yourself of rest and the simplicity
of days to come.
You must not remember the boy who played the violin
in a candlelit alley in Rome,
the legless man who was perched on a sidewalk, pulling
himself up with his flat palms,
the three young nuns coming out of the heavy church doors,
one stopping to straighten her veil, a wisp of hair coming free.

XII

Believe you do not deserve it
anyway.

Notes on Poems

Some of these poems appeared in literary magazines and journals, often in different forms; thank you to the editors: *CV2* for "3 am, march 2, 2005"; *Grain Magazine* for "unclaimed"; *The Malahat Review* for "posing for Bellocq"; *Prism International* for "Medical Inspection" and "bathing"; *Room* for "how we define voluntary."

The poem "directions for sleep" was first runner-up in *Grain*'s 21st Annual Short Grain Contest. The poetry sequence routine (comprised of the poems "Saskatoon Sanatorium, 1940," "vows, 1946," "routine, 1951," "empty, 1977," and "descent, 1983") was selected as first runner-up for *Prism International*'s 2013 Poetry Contest.

Many of the poems from the section "shadowlands" are based on paintings, literature, and historical figures.

"Ophelia swims the river" is inspired by the character of Ophelia from *Hamlet*.

Suzanne Valadon's drawings and paintings were the inspiration for "bathing" and "The Blue Room."

The work and life of Henri de Toulouse-Lautrec inspired "La Toilette," "Medical Inspection" and "Equestrienne."

Camille Claudel's life, work, and her commitment at Montdevergues Asylum inspired "how we define voluntary."

In December 1926, Agatha Christie disappeared for eleven days; she never explained her disappearance. The poem "absent in the spring" is my response to her disappearance. The title is taken from her 1944 novel of the same name.

In 1963, Sylvia Plath took her own life; six years later, Assia Wevill gassed herself and her four-year-old daughter. The poems "how would you know it was love?" and "dreamless" are my interpretations of these tragedies.

EJ Bellocq was a photographer in New Orleans in the early 20th century, his work often depicting the prostitutes in Storyville, the city's red light district. "Storyville, 1912" and "posing for Bellocq" are inspired by his life and work.

Acknowledgements

Thank you to Jane Silcott and Kim Morden for reading early drafts of this collection, in other forms and in various degrees of completion, over four long years; your thoughts were, as always, insightful and inspiring. Enormous thank you to my publisher, Karen Haughian, and my keen-eyed editor, Clarise Foster. For never-ending support, thank you to my father, Bob MacPherson, and my grandfather, Tom Rowbottom. And to Stephen Donnery for love, laughter and everything else in between.

Much of this collection was inspired by new motherhood and a profound interest in the ways in which we pass down female histories. To the late May Rowbottom and Gertrude MacPherson, without whom this collection would never have been started. For my mother, Lesley MacPherson, who gave me memories and so much more. To Taylor, who met my grandmothers and can keep those memories with her. And to my tiny, sweet girl, Nora, who did not have the chance to meet these remarkable women, but will carry on these inheritances nonetheless, and will perhaps know them through poetry.

About the Author

Andrea MacPherson, a poet and novelist, holds an MFA in Creative Writing from the University of British Columbia. She has published two novels, *When She Was Electric* (Raincoast, 2003) and *Beyond the Blue* (Random House, 2007), and two previous collections of poems, *Natural Disasters* (Palimpsest Press, 2007) and *Away* (Signature Editions, 2008). She is the reviews editor for *Event*, a past editor of *Prism International*, and teaches creative writing and literature at the University of the Fraser Valley. She lives in Cloverdale, BC.

Other books
by Andrea MacPherson

Away: Poems

Beyond the Blue

Natural Disasters

When She Was Electric

Eco-Audit
Printing this book using Rolland Opaque 50 instead of virgin fibres paper saved the following resources:

Trees	Solid Waste	Water	Air Emissions
1	16 kg	1,341 L	151 kg